Family Planning

A GUIDE FOR EXPLORING THE ISSUES

Third Edition

Charles and Elizabeth Balsam

Liguori

ONE LIGUORI DRIVE
LIGUORI MO 63057-9999

Imprimi Potest:
James Shea, C.SS.R.
Provincial, St. Louis Province
The Redemptorists

Imprimatur:
+ Edward J. O'Donnell, D.D.
Archdiocesan Administrator, Archdiocese of St. Louis

ISBN 0-89243-592-5
Library of Congress Catalog Card Number: 93-79880

Copyright © 1985, 1986, and 1994, Liguori Publications
Printed in the United States of America
02 03 04 05 06   24 23 22 21 20

The Scripture quotation is taken from the *New American Bible*, Copyright ©
1970, 1986, and 1991 by the Confraternity of Christian Doctrine, 3211 Fourth
Street, N.E., Washington, DC 20017-1194, and is used with permission. All
rights reserved.

Excerpts from *The Documents of Vatican II,* Abbott-Gallagher edition, have
been reprinted with permission of America Press, Inc., 106 West 56th Street,
New York, NY 10019. Copyright © 1966. All rights reserved.

Excerpts from *To Live in Christ Jesus,* copyright © 1976, *On the Family,*
copyright © 1981, and *On the Regulation of Birth,* copyright © 1968, by the
United States Catholic Conference, are used with permission.

To order, call 1-800-325-9521
www.liguori.org
www.catholicbooksonline.com

Cover design by Chris Sharp

———————————— **Many Thanks** ————————————

There are many people who helped us write and revise this booklet. Space does
not allow us to mention them all. However, we would like to express our sincere
appreciation and indebtedness to three special, supportive people: Rev. Albert
Moraczewski, O.P.; Joseph M. Boyle, Ph.D.; and most especially Hanna Klaus,
M.D., F.A.C.O.G.

Contents

Cooperating With God

Love is essentially a gift; and conjugal love...does not end with the couple, because it makes them capable of the greatest possible gift, the gift by which they become cooperators with God for giving life to a new human person.[1]

As baptized Christians, on your wedding day you pledge(d) to be a living sign of Christ's love for the Church. You seal this pledge in your public consent to three vows: to permanence, to fidelity, and to the openness of becoming parents. In this way, you cooperate with God's design for marital love, and your children become a living sign of your covenant.

Being "cooperators with God" involves much more than simply biological information and technological research because family planning is a faith issue. Cooperating with God is related to your perception of how God acts through you as embodied spirits.

Being "cooperators with God" also reflects your understanding of the covenant commitment of two persons in Christian marriage. We believe, therefore, that it is essential for you to obtain and discuss—as a couple—accurate information about family planning in the context of sacramental marriage.

Whether you are Catholic or not, there are additional factors that surround the question of family planning. Other issues, such as health risks and side effects, must be considered. We also want to challenge you to think about your family planning goals, shared responsibility, the gift of fertility, and the joy of having children—not just how to avoid having them.

Notes

1. Pope John Paul II, *On the Family* (The Apostolic Exhortation *Familiaris Consortio*), 1981, Part Two, 14.

Knowing the Facts

In our teaching experience, we encounter many couples who are ignorant of the most basic information about family planning methods. Many times a decision to use a particular method is made quickly, with little knowledge, understanding, or reflection. This reality has led us to include an explanation of all family planning methods in this booklet. An explanation does not imply endorsement, however. Later in this booklet we give reasons for our views and express our support of Catholic teaching concerning the moral and relational values of responsible parenthood.

Because of the potentially serious health risks of some contraceptives, doctors are required by law to provide women with a government brochure on the oral contraceptive, injectable contraceptive, contraceptive implant, and the intrauterine device (IUD) when they seek to use those methods. Regrettably, the government brochure and the vital information it contains are sometimes ignored or given little attention. Despite the doctors' responsibility, the bottom line is that patients are ultimately responsible for themselves. Doctors cannot necessarily be blamed for complications resulting from the use of the pill when patients are supposed to be aware of the risk they may be undertaking.

Some doctors or family planning agencies may not have up-to-date information about natural methods. As a result, clients may only receive information on contraceptive methods. Here again, you are responsible for finding out many of these things for yourself. In her book *The Personal Fertility Guide*, Terrie Guay says it well: "...until all the facts are known and understood, a woman is not free to make an informed choice. Ignorance is never a virtue, and choices depend not only on values but also on knowledge."[1]

This booklet provides you with an opportunity to educate yourself in an area that can affect your physical, emotional, and marital well-being. Because some contraceptives may be harmful to you, it is important to understand all of the consequences involved with any method. Natural methods are often misrepresented and misunderstood. Therefore, the most recent, up-to-date information has been compiled here in a format that attempts to be informative, understandable, and challenging.

Please note: This booklet is by no means exhaustive nor a substitute for the more detailed information that can be obtained from your doctor or natural family planning professional.

Notes

1. Terrie Guay, *The Personal Fertility Guide*, Harbor Publishing, Inc., San Francisco, CA, 1980, pp. ix-x.

Family Planning Methods

Methods of family planning fall into two basic categories: *natural* and *artificial*.

Natural methods do not use any chemical, drug, or device. They rely, rather, on the natural signs and symptoms within a woman to identify the times of fertility and infertility. The natural process of the reproductive system is left intact and undisturbed.

Modern methods of natural family planning (NFP) differ from Calendar Rhythm in this way: they are based upon the physiological signs of fertility and infertility as they occur in each and every cycle.

With a natural method, if you wish to avoid pregnancy, you agree as a couple to refrain from intercourse at the time of fertility. On the other hand, if you wish to achieve pregnancy, you continue using the method and plan intercourse at the most fertile time.

Artificial methods rely on a device, a chemical, or a drug to change and/or interfere with the normal process of the reproductive system and therefore prevent pregnancy.

The name *contraceptive* (which means a preventive to conception) is in some cases a misnomer. With the oral contraceptive, injectable contraceptive, contraceptive implant, and the intrauterine device, *conception is not always prevented.* Instead, the human embryo is unable to survive in the disturbed uterus as a result of the device or drug.

Artificial methods are not intended to help achieve pregnancy. If a pregnancy is desired, an artificial method must be discontinued.

The chart that follows is a simplified overview of the various family planning methods.

Method	Effectiveness*		Physical Side Effects and Health Risks
	Method	User-Variable	
Ovulation Method (natural)	99%	85-99%	none
Sympto-Thermal Method (natural)	99%	91-98%	none
Oral Contraceptive (the Pill) Injectable Contraceptive	99%	91-97%	nausea, vomiting, abnormal vaginal bleeding, headaches, depression, weight change, dizziness, high blood pressure, heart attack, stroke, gall bladder disease, liver tumors
Contraceptive Implant	99%	97%	abnormal vaginal bleeding, headaches, nausea, depression, weight change, acne, mood changes
Intrauterine Device (IUD)	99%	94%	heavy menstrual bleeding, cramps, painful intercourse, anemia, abnormal vaginal bleeding, pelvic infection, blood poisoning, perforation of the uterus, septic abortion, ectopic pregnancy
Diaphragm Cervical Cap	94%	92%	irritation or allergic reaction to rubber and/or spermicide, bladder infection
Spermicides	90-94%	80-85%	irritation or allergic reaction to chemicals, bladder infection
Male Condom	97%	90%	irritation or allergic reaction to rubber material

*Data on effectiveness of family planning methods taken from: J. Trussell and B. Vaughn, "Contraceptive Failure, Method-Related Discontinuation and Resumption of the Use Results from the 1995 NSFG," in *Family Planning Perspectives*, March/April 1999 [31/2] 64-72; and Fu.H.etal, "Contraceptive Failure Rates: New Estimates from the 1995 National Survey of Family Growth," in *Family Planning Perspectives*, March/April 1999 [31/2] 56-63. Refer to pages 23 to 25 of this booklet for a further explanation of effectiveness rates.

Natural Family Planning

Ovulation Method

The Ovulation Method of natural family planning is sometimes called the Billings Method (for Drs. John and Evelyn Billings of Australia). This method teaches a couple to identify the fertile and infertile days in a woman's cycle by observing the changes in the cervical mucus secretion.

The cervix is at the base of a woman's uterus. Mucus is secreted by the cervix directly prior to and at the time of ovulation.

The couple using the Ovulation Method keeps a daily chart of the woman's vaginal sensations and the color and consistency of any mucus secretion. The sensations and type of mucus observed tell the woman when she is fertile. If pregnancy is to be avoided, continence (refraining from intercourse) is necessary during the fertile days of the cycle. Continence is a mutual effort for both the man and the woman of which neither partner has to bear the sole responsibility for avoiding pregnancy.

It is necessary to learn the Ovulation Method from an instructor (often a couple) who is qualified to teach the method and who has personal experience with it.

The Ovulation Method can be used successfully in any reproductive situation: regular, irregular, or anovular cycles; while breast-feeding; and during premenopause.

Method Effectiveness: 99%

Side Effects: None

Health Factors: None

Effect on Ability to Have Children: Because the Ovulation Method does not use any drugs, devices, or chemicals, it leaves the reproductive system of both the male and female undisturbed and does not endanger the fertility of the couple. Since the Ovulation Method identifies the time of fertility, it can be used in an effort to achieve pregnancy, as well as to avoid pregnancy. For couples who have "low fertility" or some difficulty in conceiving, the Ovulation Method may be helpful to achieving pregnancy.

Sympto-Thermal Method

The Sympto-Thermal Method of natural family planning combines the use of the Ovulation Method with the basal body temperature and other indicators of fertility. The cervical mucus is observed and, upon waking in the morning, the woman takes a reading of her temperature with a special calibrated thermometer.

A woman's basal body temperature rises after ovulation. When it has remained high for three consecutive days, this fact signals that the fertile phase of the cycle has passed.

With the Sympto-Thermal Method some aspects of Calendar Rhythm may also be used, and actual changes in the cervix may be observed and noted. At times, the basal body temperature may have limited use—for example, when cycles are anovular or irregular; during months when breast-feeding is done; or during premenopause. In such situations, observation of the cervical mucus is very important.

With the Sympto-Thermal Method, continence (refraining from intercourse) during the fertile time is necessary to avoid pregnancy. Instruction by a qualified teacher is essential to learn the method.

The Sympto-Thermal Method can be used successfully in any reproductive situation: with regular, irregular, or anovular cycles; during the time of breast-feeding; and during premenopause.

Method Effectiveness: 99%

Side Effects: None

Health Factors: None

Effect on Ability to Have Children: Because the Sympto-Thermal Method does not disturb or endanger the fertility of the couple, there is no adverse effect on the ability to have children. By observing the cervical mucus secretion, a couple can identify the time of fertility and actually use this knowledge to achieve pregnancy. For couples who have difficulty in conceiving, this information may be helpful to achieving pregnancy.

From a Woman's Heart

By Elizabeth Balsam

I first began learning about Natural Family Planning when I was nineteen years old. My mom gave me a book that briefly described the Ovulation Method, which made me eager to learn more about my fertility signs.

I was drawn to NFP for several reasons. First, I love the outdoors, and NFP appealed to my sense of being connected to nature. Second, I had painful menstrual bleeds and hoped that a better understanding of my cycles would help me anticipate the arrival of my periods. Finally, I was somewhat aware of how contraceptives worked and was curious about a method that would not mess up my body. All of these reasons were, at first, me-centered. I had not yet considered NFP in relation to another person.

Cycle after cycle of fertility awareness began to have an effect on me. This was *me*, a wonderfully designed member of God's creation. The pine trees and the creeks and the stars had nothing over this amazing aspect of me: fertility. I was delighted to discover that there were actual signs in me that enabled me to know and understand my fertility. Fertility became familiar and very *real* to me. The "curse" of the menstrual cycle was transformed into some-thing holy and wonderful. I realized that I am even more wonder-fully made than the stately loblolly pines and the starlike twinkle of Venus. Spiritually, the awareness of my fertility cycles and the appreciation of how I am made brought me closer to God and creation.

My husband and I met while in college. When marriage became part of our discussions, I nervously broached the subject of Natural Family Planning. How would he react? Would he think I was crazy to want to use NFP in marriage? Would NFP really work to prevent pregnancy? Despite my questions and doubts, using a contraceptive method in our marriage was unacceptable to me. I felt very much the same as Juli Loesch: "...as regards my own waterways, which, more than any of the wild rivers of the world, have a right to be what they are: clean, that is, not spiked with toxic chemicals....There are some things in this universe that are sacred. Me, for instance."[1]

So, I showed my future husband the charts I had been keeping of my cycles. I tried to explain to him what I was observing about my fertility. I located a class on NFP and we attended it together. I tried to explain why I believed NFP would be better for us than contraception. Gradually, *my* fertility was becoming *our* fertility. We talked mostly in terms of "health" and "nature" and "effectiveness."

We married, planning the wedding date so that our honeymoon would occur during the infertile time of my cycle. Month after month, the use of natural family planning began to have an effect on me—and my husband. The first couple of years, we chose to use NFP to avoid pregnancy. Refraining from intercourse during our fertile time was not always easy.

My husband's determination to lovingly live NFP in the early years of our marriage made a great impression upon me. It was clear to both of us that I did not have to alter myself, specifically my fertility, to be loved by him. The love we have for each other has been shaped and strengthened by our shared responsibility and mutual commitment to family planning.

Natural family planning has an exciting advantage over contraception, and I looked forward to the day when we would begin a family. Our potential as husband and wife to conceive a child and to lovingly welcome that child into our home is a God-given blessing. It is the greatest possible gift that a married couple can share with each other. As a young married woman, I became increasingly attuned to the possible fruit of our embodied love. "It is not unusual for couples [who use NFP] to be so enchanted by the way that nature works that they consciously choose to have a child."[2]

I will never forget the first time that my husband and I became "two in one flesh" during our fertile time with the high hopes of conceiving a child. We felt a sense of oneness with the creative mysteries of God. Mary Shivanandan writes that NFP, for some couples, releases a "deep wellspring of creativity."[3]

With time, I have come to understand that fertility acceptance through NFP can encompass a wide range of situations. For some couples, it may mean welcoming a "surprise" pregnancy and allowing God to be revealed in the child. Other couples may have to face some form of infertility, either temporary or permanent. For my husband and me, it meant living with a fertility that was impaired by endometriosis (a disease of the uterine lining). Yet, NFP prepared us even for that. We faced the challenge together, with love and faith in God. I slowly learned to accept a fertility that was uniquely different from what I knew at age nineteen.

As a wife and mother, I am grateful for all that NFP has done to enrich my life. Fertility cycles are, in circular repetition, like a crown of flowers, curling and weaving until it is years old, heavy and fragrant. This splendid crown may include bare branches, wild grasses, and unexpected blossoms. Each cycle clings to the next, and like the seasons of the year, contains memories, struggles, and joys. It has been a blessing to share this wreath of my cycles with my husband.

God has generously provided spouses with the gift of fertility and the ability to understand and embrace it. Fertility is an integral part of God's complementary design for man and woman. God, I suspect, is pleased when married couples come to know and revere their fertility. For it is through this life-giving potential that God's image continues in the world.

Notes

1. Juli Loesch, *Commonweal,* October 18, 1985, Vol. CXLL, No. 18.
2. Mary Shivanandan, *Challenge to Love,* KM Associates, Bethesda, Maryland, 1979, p. 76.
3. Ibid., p. 74.

Artificial Methods

Oral Contraceptives

"The pill" refers to any of the oral contraceptives. The most widely used is the combination pill containing two synthetic female hormones: estrogen and progestin. The other two oral contraceptives are the minipill, which contains only progestin, and the triphasic pill, which varies the level of hormones in a woman's body. The pills must be taken regularly and exactly as instructed. The contraceptive pill is a prescription drug. Depo-Provera is a progestin-only contraceptive available by injection.

For the most part, the pill prevents ovulation from occurring in the woman. It also causes a thick mucus at the cervix, which acts as a barrier to sperm. In the case where ovulation does occur and the sperm do penetrate the mucus, conception may result. Due to the hostile environment that the pill creates in the womb, however, the human embryo may be unable to implant in the wall of the uterus. (The result may be a very early abortion indistinguishable from a normal menstrual flow. In this, the woman is unaware that she is even pregnant.) The minipill and the triphasic pill are less reliable than the combination pill in suppressing ovulation. The injectable contraceptive alters the uterine lining to prevent implantation.

A woman using the pill is advised to have a Pap test about every six months.

Method Effectiveness: 99%

Side Effects: Oral contraceptives may cause nausea, vomiting, cramps, weight change, nervousness, depression, dizziness, loss of hair, vaginal infections, rash, headaches, abnormal vaginal bleeding, and water retention. Oral contraceptives may cause high blood pressure and may increase the risk of gallbladder disease. Pill users have a greater risk of heart attack and stroke. Contact-lens wearers may notice a change in vision or some discomfort when wearing their lenses. Some drugs interact with oral contraceptives, making the pill less effective or causing abnormal vaginal bleeding. Antibiotics, barbiturates, and antiseizure medications are some of the drugs known to interact with oral contraceptives. Side effects of the injectable contraceptive are the same as the pill, with a higher risk of unpredictable vaginal bleeding or amenorrhea (no menstruation).

Health Factors: Women with a history of heart disease, stroke, blood clots, unexplained vaginal bleeding, cancer of the breast or uterus, or liver tumors should not use the pill. Women who smoke dramatically increase their risk of heart attack and stroke when using the pill. A woman who may be pregnant should not use the pill because it increases the risk of defect of the baby. Health problems such as migraine headaches, depression, heart disease, kidney disease, asthma, high blood pressure, diabetes, or epilepsy may be made worse with use of the pill.

Effect on Ability to Have Children: When a woman stops taking the pill in order to become pregnant, there may be a delay before she is actually able to become pregnant. To allow the woman's reproductive system to return to normal, a couple should wait a short time—probably several months after stopping the pill—before attempting to become pregnant. The injectable contraceptive may delay the return of fertility for up to twelve months after the injection is stopped. Studies have shown that drugs in the pill appear in the breast milk of nursing mothers. The long-range effect on the infant is not known.

Contraceptive Implant

The contraceptive implant is a hormonal device that has recently been made available in the United States. The device consists of six small, flexible rods implanted just under the skin along the inside of the upper arm of a woman. The implants are inserted with local anesthesia by a doctor. There may be some pain during insertion and following; soreness, swelling, and bruises on the arm may occur for about a week. The contour of the implanted rods may be visible under the skin, and scar tissue may develop on the arm area.

The implants are hollow rods containing a synthetic form of progestin that is slowly released into a woman's body and prevents ovulation in about half of her menstrual cycles. The hormone in the implant also causes a thick mucus at the cervix that acts as a barrier to sperm. In cycles where ovulation does occur and conception results, the human embryo may be unable to imbed in the wall of the uterus due to the hostile environment the implant creates. (The result is a very early abortion indistinguishable from a normal menstrual flow. In this, the woman is unaware that she has conceived.)

The contraceptive implant is intended to provide long-term pregnancy prevention and can be effective for up to five years. The effectiveness rate of the contraceptive implant is somewhat lower for women who are overweight.

Method Effectiveness: 99%

Side Effects: The most common side effect associated with the implant is changes in menstrual patterns, such as prolonged, excessive, or irregular bleeding. Amenorrhea (no menstruation) may also occur. Other side effects include headaches, nausea, depression, mood changes, increased appetite, changes in weight, and acne.

Health Factors: Women who have abnormal vaginal bleeding, liver disease, known or suspected breast cancer, and thrombophlebitis should not use the contraceptive implant. A woman who believes she may be pregnant should not use the implant because it increases the risk of defect of the baby. Health problems such as migraine headaches or depression may be made worse by the use of the implant.

Effect on Ability to Have Children: When a woman has the implants removed from her arm, healthy fertility usually will return promptly.

Intrauterine Device (IUD)

The intrauterine device (IUD) is a small plastic device that is placed in the uterus of the woman through the cervix. Insertion by a physician is necessary. After insertion, no further care is needed except to see that the device remains in place. The user can check herself, but she should be checked at least once a year by her doctor.

The IUD may cause pain or discomfort when inserted, and afterward may cause cramps and a menstrual flow that is heavier than usual.

Since the IUD does not prevent ovulation from occurring, conception could happen in almost every cycle. The IUD seems to interfere in some manner with the implantation of the human embryo in the wall of the uterus. (The result may be a very early abortion indistinguishable from a normal menstrual flow. In this, the woman is unaware that she is even pregnant.)

It is somewhat difficult for a woman to obtain an intrauterine device because many IUDs have been removed from the U.S. market.

Method Effectiveness: 99%

Side Effects: IUD users may experience heavy menstrual bleeding, cramps, and painful intercourse. Major complications, which are infrequent, include anemia, pregnancy outside of the uterus, pelvic infections, perforation of the uterus or cervix, and septic abortion. A woman who experiences very heavy or irregular bleeding while using the IUD should consult her physician; removal of the IUD may be necessary to prevent anemia. Women susceptible to pelvic infection are more prone to infection while using the IUD. Serious complications can occur if the woman becomes pregnant while an IUD is in place; there is an increased chance of tubal pregnancy or miscarriage and infection, both potentially fatal problems. An IUD user who believes she may be pregnant should consult her doctor immediately. If pregnancy is confirmed, the IUD may have to be removed. Although it rarely happens, the IUD can pierce the wall of the uterus while it is being inserted, in which case surgery is required to remove it. The risk of tubal pregnancy is greater with the use of the IUD, and the risk increases the longer the IUD is used.

Health Factors: Before having the IUD inserted, a woman should tell her doctor if she has had any of the following: cancer or other abnormalities of the uterus or cervix; bleeding between periods or heavy menstrual flows; infection of the uterus, cervix, or pelvis; prior IUD use; recent pregnancy; abortion or miscarriage; uterine surgery; venereal disease; severe menstrual cramps; anemia; fainting attacks; unexplained genital bleeding or vaginal discharge; suspicious or abnormal Pap test; uterine fibroids; history of ectopic pregnancy.

Effect on Ability to Have Children: Pelvic infection in some IUD users may result in their future inability to have children. Woman who have never had children are usually discouraged from using the IUD.

Diaphragm/Cervical Cap

The diaphragm is a shallow cup of thin rubber stretched over a flexible ring. Before intercourse, a sperm-killing cream or jelly is applied to both sides of the diaphragm, which the woman then places inside the vagina. The diaphragm covers the opening of the uterus, at the cervix, thus preventing the sperm from entering the uterus. The spermicide also helps to disable and destroy the sperm.

Sizing and fitting of the diaphragm must be done by a doctor, and requires yearly checkups. Size and fit should also be checked if the woman gains or loses more than ten pounds, and after pregnancy or pelvic surgery.

The cervical cap is similar to the diaphragm except that it is a smaller, thimble-shaped cup and is held snugly in place over the cervix by suction. A spermicide, which helps prevent the sperm from entering the uterus, is used with the cap. The cervical cap must be specially fitted by a doctor.

The diaphragm and the cervical cap are reusable for up to two years and should be regularly inspected for holes, tears, or puckering.

Method Effectiveness: 94%

Side Effects: There may be an allergic reaction to the rubber of the diaphragm/cervical cap or to the spermicide. Some irritation or discomfort may occur. There may be an increase in vaginal odor and susceptibility to bladder infection.

Health Factors: The cervical cap should not be used by women with a history of abnormal Pap tests.

Effect on Ability to Have Children: None

Spermicides

Several brands of vaginal foam, cream, jelly, or suppositories can be used without a diaphragm. They must be placed inside the vagina before intercourse. At the opening of the uterus, spermicides form a barrier that prevents sperm from reaching the egg. Spermicides disable, damage, and destroy the sperm.

No prescription is necessary for the purchase of spermicides.

Some brands of spermicides are not as effective as others in preventing pregnancy. For example, instead of foaming up, some suppositories may remain intact and fall out of the vagina. The aerosol foams are the most effective of the chemical spermicides.

Method Effectiveness: 90-94%

Side Effects: Some burning or irritation of the vagina or penis may occur due to an allergic reaction to the chemicals in spermicides. There may be an increase in vaginal odor and susceptibility to bladder infection.

Health Factors: None

Effect on Ability to Have Children: None

Condom

The condom is a thin sheath of rubber or processed lamb cecum that fits over the penis. The condom must be fit in place over the penis before any genital contact with the woman.

No prescription is required for the purchase of condoms.

The condom prevents the sperm from entering the woman's vagina so that it cannot fertilize the egg. Care must be taken in the use of the condom since it can slip or tear during use or sperm can spill from the condom upon withdrawal from the vagina.

Method Effectiveness: 97%

Side Effects: Occasionally, there may be an allergic reaction to the rubber material, causing some irritation.

Health Factors: None

Effect on Ability to Have Children: None

Methods That Are Not Reliable

- Douching after intercourse is unreliable as a means of avoiding pregnancy. If the conditions are favorable in the woman's body, sperm can travel to meet the egg within minutes of ejaculation.
- Not all forms of breast-feeding provide for extended infertility after childbirth. In general, breast-feeding may delay the return of fertility in many women, but certain kinds of breast-feeding ("partial") do little to suppress ovulation. In some cases, a nursing mother could conceive within several months of delivery. The return of fertility after childbirth depends greatly on the *type* of breast-feeding/mothering used. Some forms of breast-feeding ("total" or "ecological") more completely suppress ovulation for an extended length of time.
- *Coitus interruptus* is the difficult and often frustrating practice of withdrawing the penis from the vagina just before ejaculation. It is unreliable as a means of avoiding pregnancy because a few drops of very potent fluid may leave the penis before ejaculation and before withdrawal.
- For most women, Calendar Rhythm is not a reliable way to avoid pregnancy because some irregularity may occur in a woman's cycles. Calendar Rhythm is based on calculations from previous cycles with no regard for the present one. A woman could conceive at a time when she thinks she is infertile.

A Word
About Effectiveness

There is some confusion among couples and medical professionals alike about the effectiveness of natural methods of family planning. Many still think of natural methods as only Calendar Rhythm or, possibly, Basal Body Temperature.

Confusion, ignorance, and misinformation about the effectiveness of modern methods of natural family planning mean that many couples never give it serious consideration. This is very unfortunate, not only because natural methods are, in fact, reliable but because they can do so much to enrich a marriage.

On page 8 of this booklet, statistics for "method effectiveness" are given for both natural and artificial methods. A method-effectiveness rate is determined by the number of pregnancies that occur in proportion to the total number of couples using that method, even when the guidelines for pregnancy avoidance have been properly understood and faithfully followed.

Method-effectiveness figures are usually high and illustrate the reliability of the method *when used correctly* to avoid pregnancy. Keep in mind that *none of the methods listed in this booklet are 100 percent effective* in avoiding pregnancy. All methods carry some slight possibility of pregnancy, even when they are used strictly according to the guidelines.

Besides the slight possibility of a pregnancy occurring when a method is used correctly, pregnancies during use of a family planning method can also occur for other reasons:

- The couple does not understand how to use a method.
- The couple knows how to use a method but disregards the guidelines for avoiding pregnancy.
- The couple seeks to achieve pregnancy.

The last reason applies only to the actual use of natural methods of family planning. Artificial methods are intended solely for the avoidance of pregnancy and cannot help achieve pregnancy. On the other hand, natural methods can be used either to avoid *or* to achieve pregnancy. The complete and accurate definition of true family planning, which includes having children, is more fully realized in natural methods.

The percentage rates for "user-variable effectiveness" (see the chart on page 8) for both natural and artificial methods are determined by the number of pregnancies that occur in proportion to the total number of couples using that method under the circumstances described in the first two reasons. The first reason means that pregnancies may occur because the couple did not seek or receive proper instruction in how to use a method. This does *not* mean that the method is unreliable, but that the couple did not have correct information about how to use the method to avoid pregnancy.

When a couple knows how to apply the guidelines of a method to avoid pregnancy, there are many complex reasons why they disregard the rules. Often the couple is ambivalent about whether or not to have a baby. They may not have clearly discussed their goals and plans for the future. Couples may "take a chance" with the use of a method or become careless in using the method. Sometimes the subconscious desire for a child is very strong and causes a couple not to carefully follow the method guidelines to avoid pregnancy. These examples illustrate some of the variables that contribute to the way a couple uses a method. The motivation of each couple is unique and different. Pregnancies that occur under these circumstances do not mean that the method is unreliable, but that the couple chooses to disregard the guidelines for pregnancy avoidance—for whatever reason.

Natural family planning is often said to be ineffective, based on user-variable effectiveness rates (which are lower than method-effectiveness rates). One reason for this is that medical professionals, among others, falsely assume that couples are unwilling or unable to lovingly practice the continence necessary for the avoidance of pregnancy. Dr. Hanna Klaus, a gynecologist, natural family planning expert, and Medical Missionary Sister, responds in the following way: "To read use-effectiveness figures as meaning that clients either cannot learn the method, or will not practice it consistently and therefore have an unplanned pregnancy, is to make condescending assumptions about human intelligence or freedom, and to attempt to reduce complex personal decision making to a demographic figure."[1]

The many couples who successfully use natural family planning methods to avoid or achieve pregnancy are testimony to the capacity of human beings to understand and integrate their fertility into their marriage. Natural family planning means accepting yourself, your spouse, and your joint fertility. It means an openness to living and expressing your relationship over time through children. Natural methods are true and effective family planning.

Notes

1. Hanna Klaus, M.D., *Intercom*, "The Distinction Between Method and User Failure of NFP Methods," March 1980, p. 12.

For Men Only

by Charles Balsam

My experience of marital sexuality has been a mixture of pain and redemption. The pain comes, in part, from the natural struggle of two lovers to "tune in" to each other's needs. It also comes from my own immaturity and some unrealistic expectations. When these go unspoken and are not dealt with mutually, the struggle seems to be compounded. Love takes time. Love needs bridges, not barriers. Sexually, the biggest barrier I brought to my marriage was my hesitancy to risk. I believe the form of family planning we chose has helped me to accept myself and to seek a deeper union with my wife. This has been redemptive, for I experience God's love through my wife in our struggle to love each other unconditionally and sacrificially.

My wife once told me that she might not have married me if I had insisted on a chemical form of family planning. That's tough love! She was concerned with her personal integrity and the interpersonal dynamics of our relationship. She had been charting her natural signs of fertility for over two years. For her to take full responsibility for our fertility through contraception would have been to diminish her self-gift. It took me several years to realize the meaning of this. In other words, she taught me something important about total giving and accepting of each other in marriage.

Living NFP has not always been easy. I am not speaking of the fear of unplanned pregnancy. I am speaking of continence, that is, refraining from intercourse to postpone conception during the phases of our cycle when we are both fertile.

Some criticize abstinence or continence as unnatural and thus view NFP as too difficult. I think the difficulty lies in what continence can reveal. I discovered that I had placed more emphasis on genital intimacy than relational intimacy. Besides providing us with the possibility of invoking new life, sexual intercourse (genital intimacy) celebrates relational intimacy.

In and of itself, sex does not create marital intimacy. In fact, sometimes sex isn't intimate at all. I have found this to be true most often when we are not relationally intimate. Using a chemical or a mechanical contraceptive would represent another kind of intimacy barrier. For us to alter or destroy our fertility would also destroy the power of intercourse to signify total self-giving. Retaining the full meaning of intercourse is important to us.

This experience of learning and living NFP has caused me to reflect on myself as a rather typical, twentieth-century American male. While it is natural for persons to yearn for intimacy and affection, I do not believe I was socialized to be relationally intimate. Stereotypically, men have been raised to be analytical, detached, and performance oriented.

In a way, becoming relationally intimate with my wife has been "unnatural" for me. Thus, I think men have to *learn* to be intimate beyond the genital expression of marital love. In my own struggle, I have had to become more emotionally intimate and more vulnerable—two qualities that most women want in their relationship with their spouse. It is *this* learning process, not continence, which I believe many find to be "unnatural" and perhaps makes living NFP difficult for some couples.

Continence does me a favor. It provides me with a "rhythmic" opportunity to make sure it is not only sex, but more so love and intimacy that bind me to my wife. This is why we assert that contraception is chauvinistic. Contraception isolates the responsibility for transmitting life to one spouse (usually the wife), and it reinforces what I call the Playboy playmate-fantasy caricature of woman: sexually precocious, available, and sterile. Because a woman can become pregnant, in this caricature she and her sexuality are deemed inferior, and males continue to see her primarily as a sex object. Males continue to be rescued from integrating their own sexuality into their development and from viewing women as persons. Contraception (and abortion) are not worthy of her dignity as one image of God in the world.

Of course, the other caricature—barefoot and pregnant—is also an affront to her dignity. Modern methods of fertility acceptance (NFP) are an antidote to either caricature. When mutually learned, lovingly lived, and applied according to the goals of a couple, NFP promotes the equality and dignity of husband and wife. Contraception and abortion undermine this strength, a point many feminists seem to overlook.

Though difficult at times, integrating our fertility into our marriage has strengthened us individually and as a couple. If I had been told this before we married, I would not have believed it. I am thankful to have a spouse who loves me and herself enough to demand that I love her in a way that Christian marriage requires.

Thus, fertility acceptance (NFP) not only reminds me of the interpersonal nature of procreation, it is a constant reminder that genital intimacy belongs in the context of relational intimacy. The periodic tension that sometimes comes with continence leads us to frequently examine our relationship, our needs, our communication, and the quality of our intimacy and affection. As a male, that is extremely important, given my natural tendency to overemphasize the quality of the genital relationship.

Can I promise anything beneficial for couples considering or choosing NFP? Yes, depending on the quality of their relationship. NFP has helped me mature, though I have a long way to go. NFP has challenged me to question my assumptions about woman as mate and lover, and begin to appreciate the "feminine" aspects of myself. It has taught me the beauty of the female menstrual cycle. It has called me to cherish my wife rather than simply desire her. NFP has taught me that fertility is an integral, interpersonal power to invoke new life and participate in the creativity of God. NFP has challenged me to accept and revere our fertility as we have found it, and more fully accept the gift of each other in Christian marriage.

Shared Decision,
Shared Responsibility

Couples frequently make mutual decisions and share responsibilities about finances, parenting, housing, spousal roles, household chores, family holidays, and the like. Until recently, family planning was viewed as the sole responsibility of the wife and her doctor, often leaving out the husband. Christian marriage is an intimate partnership of life and love, a sacrament of mutual and total self-giving. Partnership calls for shared decisions and shared responsibilities.

Natural family planning best exemplifies this description of Christian marriage. Both husband and wife share the responsibility for fertility and decisions about family planning.

Fertility is a gift from God, and you are called to be generous with this gift. Family size is not just an issue of economics but also a matter of faith.

Perhaps the following questions will identify some of the values you bring to your relationship:

- To what is God calling us in our marriage?
- How may children do we hope to have?
- How generous can we be with life?
- How do we value children in relation to material things: money, possessions, social status?
- How important is the physical, psychological, or spiritual impact of a family planning method on our relationship?
- Can we remain open to these questions throughout our marriage?

As a couple, your decision making about family planning requires prayer, a reverence for and an openness to God's creative presence in your lives. You must be able to talk honestly and lovingly about the value you place on children and on a Christian family. It is important to remember that conception is a logical and beautiful result of your covenant love. Children are the living manifestation of your love in-the-flesh.

We urge you to reflect upon and discuss all these issues in a faith context. We are called to be generative and fruitful people. Fertility is one avenue through which we join our will to the creative intentions of God. It is the way we continue to call into being other human persons who become the image and likeness of God in the world. If fertility is an integral part of human dignity, then it follows that every child is a unique, unrepeatable person. Children represent our belief that life is worth living, and that the fullness of the kingdom of God is yet to come.

Page 45 of this booklet contains a worksheet. It is an opportunity for you as a couple to discuss family planning, your relationship as sexual persons, and your expectations within the context of Christian marriage. We hope that this booklet, along with your responses to the worksheet, contributes to an honest, "faith-full" understanding as you make mutual, conscientious decisions about family planning.

Finally, we offer a prayer for Christian parenthood. We urge you to pray it frequently as a couple and reflect on its meaning, most especially when you feel called to cooperate with God's creative love in bringing new life and new hope into the world.

God our Creator, all parenthood comes from you. Allow us to share in that power which is yours alone. Help us to see in the children you send us living signs of your presence in our home. Bless our love and make it fruitful so that new voices may join ours in praise of you, new hearts love you, and new lives bear witness to you.

Author unknown

What Does the Catholic Church Teach?

Human life is sacred: From its very inception, it reveals the creating hand of God.

Pope John XXIII

Most people are aware of the fact that the Roman Catholic Church does not endorse all family planning methods presented in this booklet. This section is an explanation of the reasoning behind Church teaching.

We urge you to read this section carefully and with an open heart. It is important to realize that the Church's concern for the moral aspects of family planning is not simply a set of rules. Church teaching is ensured by Jesus' promise of the guidance of the Spirit. Even though there is not adequate space here to go into great detail, a few remarks are in order.

You will make many responsible decisions about how you spend money or time, how you accumulate material goods, and so forth. But your fertility is about the procreation and perpetuation of the image of God (in a new human being) in the world. It is directly related to and empowered by God, who is the Author of marital sexuality. This is why the Church has been concerned about how couples live their fertility.

In continuity with Church teaching, the Second Vatican Council (1962-1965) asserted that the manner in which human life is transmitted must be determined by objective standards. These standards are "based on the nature of the human person and his acts" in order to "preserve the *full sense* of *mutual self-giving* and *human procreation* in the context of true love."[1] The phrase "full sense" means that conjugal intercourse, the language of marital love, is the symbol and expression of a covenant relationship—an open-ended, vulnerable commitment to an exclusive, life-giving marital union. Thus, we are speaking primarily of the *meanings* of intercourse as well as its potential "effects"—unity and parenthood. Let us briefly focus, then, on these two fundamental aspects of which the Council spoke: the nature of the human person, in light of the call to self-giving that is marriage, and the nature of conjugal intercourse.

The Human Person

Our Christian faith tells us that sexuality, our uniqueness as male or female, is God's gift to us. Pope John Paul II, citing Genesis 2:23-24, says that man and woman are created for unity. They become "one flesh" through a choice, the free gift of themselves. Christian tradition holds that a sacramental marriage begins when two persons express their consent to give and receive the person of the other. This mutual consent, spoken in the vows, is the forming of an "intimate partnership of married life and love...structured...on the model of His [Christ's] union with the Church."[2] This consent means commitment to the primary and equally important meanings of marriage—the procreation and education of children and the unity of the spouses.

In the light of mutual consent and self-giving, sexuality serves human life and human relationships. The marital relationship is fundamentally a commitment of the whole person—mind and heart, body and spirit. For Pope John Paul, sexuality and the human person are one reality. He speaks of the person as an *"incarnate spirit*...a soul which expresses itself in a body....Love includes the human body, and the body is made a sharer in spiritual love."

He adds that "sexuality...is by no means something purely biological, but concerns the *innermost being* of the human person...."[3] Since human fertility is designed to procreate a human person, it is *not merely* a physical function. Fertility must also be seen as a part of personal identity, relational values, and the gift of the whole person to another in the covenant of marriage.

Conjugal Intercourse

Marital intercourse is a natural sacrament. It is a sign of the wisdom of God's design for human persons. It is a symbol, an expression of two human beings who have vowed to openness, the vulnerability, the *mutual self-giving* of covenant love.

There are two inherent meanings in the marriage act: the procreative and the unitive. The *key* issue is the Church's concern with the morality of deliberately removing or altering the procreative meaning. To intervene, to remove the procreative meaning/potential of intercourse, is to change the *interpersonal and unitive* nature of this loving act.

Is the Church Inconsistent?

According to method effectiveness studies cited earlier in this booklet, it is clear that modern methods of natural family planning are as effective (or more effective) in avoiding pregnancy as artificial methods of birth control. After studying this data, some people assume that natural methods are simply an alternate form of contraception. They further conclude that the Church is inconsistent in promoting only natural methods of fertility acceptance while condemning artificial methods that have the same result.

It is true that in both cases the probable effect—avoiding pregnancy—can be the same. There is a fundamental difference, however, between the two forms of family planning.

It is wrongly supposed that Church teaching opposes contraception because it is used to avoid pregnancy, or because it is most often artificial. Avoiding pregnancy can be good, responsible, or even necessary for married couples. The Church is convinced, however, that certain ways of avoiding pregnancy are morally flawed. These methods compromise the very meaning of marriage and marital intercourse. The use of contraception is an attempt to alter fertility and marital intercourse by eliminating its procreative meaning and trivializing the promise of total self-giving and mutual acceptance.

Couples who choose artificial methods of birth control are making a statement about the value and the meaning of procreation in relation to their marital love. By their action, they imply that conception is merely a biological process and that the birth control method affects only their reproductive capacity. They can lose sight of the fact that as human persons they are a wondrous unity of body and spirit. Bodies do not procreate, persons do! This is why Church teaching stresses that procreation is not merely a biological function *and* that fertility should be accepted by couples in accordance with God's design. One author explains this by stating:

> In the marital act, husband and wife are "speaking" through their body language....They are not simply "using" their bodies as objects....The truth of the marital act is that it is a reciprocal gift of one's total self. It is a gift which, being total, necessarily includes the procreative potential. Since fertility is an integral element of each spouse, it must be given and received (in so far as it is present) in the marital act....
>
> To remove the procreation dimension...is to introduce the language of rejection and non-acceptance into the act. The marital act is then reduced to an act of manipulation and acceptance-only-with-some-reservations.[4]

In other words, couples willingly attempt to eliminate God's creative design from their act of love, from the gift of fertility, and from the goodness of their procreative potential. Their action "is directly aimed against the realization of the procreative good. One is simply not declining to promote that good; one is taking positive steps directly against it."[5] To depersonalize fertility risks depersonalizing total self-gift.

On the other hand, couples who use natural methods of family planning can be said to both accept and integrate their joint fertility into their covenant love, symbolized by the sex act. They do not reject God's creative presence in intercourse. By avoiding fertile intercourse, "the couple is simply not performing an action whose nature is ordained to elicit God's creative act. God is still present, still respected, but no invitation is sent him that would invite his presence in the specific form of being a creator of new life."[6]

By contrast, contraception sends the message that God's creative presence is not valued and that fertility is a biological "problem" rather than a personal gift to be respected as a blessing from God. The Church teaches that couples who practice natural methods can have intercourse during naturally infertile phases and still not be making a conscious choice against the good of procreation. These naturally infertile (noncontraceptive) acts of intercourse still have a procreative *meaning* and value, even though, *due to God's design*, they do not have a procreative *capacity* or result.

To say it another way, couples who employ fertility-acceptance methods (natural family planning) acknowledge God's creative power and do not redesign or block it. By their periodic continence, they responsibly refrain from employing this power in a given cycle or cycles. They do not reject God's creative presence in their fertility, but foster and respect the basic human good of procreation whether engaging in or abstaining from intercourse. Such couples understand that they bring themselves entirely to the sex act. Nothing is done to render sex sterile, make it incomplete, or prevent implantation of a fertilized ovum (a developing human being).

The Church's support for natural methods affirms its teaching that marriage is the mutual giving and receiving of two persons in Christ. This means that the reciprocal giving and receiving is not just spiritual or psychological but also physical, of which fertility is a part. Natural family planning fosters this integral understanding of Christian marriage. Through a fertility-acceptance lifestyle, a married couple affirms the values of personal, bodily, and spiritual integrity, and embrace mutual self-giving in union with the Creator and his design.

Therefore, if Pope John Paul's description of the human person is correct and if covenant love is the mutual self-giving of two *whole* persons, it follows that contraception is a contradiction. It attempts to eliminate the procreative meaning of marital love from the symbol of self-giving. It trivializes sex and undermines the covenant promises of marriage, namely the *complete* sharing of self and life with each other.

This quotation from Pope John Paul summarizes the ideas presented in this section:

> ...the innate language that expresses the total reciprocal self-giving of husband and wife is overlaid, through contraception, by an objectively contradictory language, namely, that of not giving oneself totally to the other. This leads...to a falsification of the inner truth of conjugal love, which is called upon to give itself in personal totality.
>
> When, instead, by means of recourse to periods of infertility, the couple respect the inseparable connection between the unitive and procreative meanings of human sexuality, they are acting as "ministers" of God's plan and they "benefit from" their sexuality according to the original dynamism of "total" self-giving, without manipulation or alteration.
>
> In the light of the experience of many couples and of the data provided by the different human sciences, theological reflection is able to perceive and...study further the difference...between contraception and recourse to the rhythm [here the pope is referring to NFP] of the cycle: It is a difference which is much wider and deeper than is usually thought, one which involves in the final analysis two irreconcilable concepts of the human person and of human sexuality. The choice of the natural rhythms [here the pope is referring to NFP] involves accepting the cycle of the person, that is, the woman, and thereby accepting

dialogue, reciprocal respect, shared responsibility and self-control....In this way sexuality is respected and promoted in its truly and fully human dimension and is never "used" as an "object" that, by breaking the personal unity of soul and body, strikes at God's creation itself at the level of the deepest interaction of nature and person.[7]

Pope John Paul addresses many deep and complex issues in his writing. It requires much prayer, patience, and reflection to fully grasp the values to which he is pointing. The following chart demonstrates the differences between the two mentalities:

Fertility Acceptance (NFP)	Contraception
1. Accepts fertility, integrating it into mutual self-giving	1. Nonacceptance by altering or destroying fertility; disintegration
2. Body as incarnate person; act through it	2. Body as subpersonal; act upon it
3. Accepts God's design by exercising dominion (stewardship)	3. Redesign creation through manipulation (domination)
4. Mutual	4. Chauvinistic or sexist
5. Behaviorally procreative or nonprocreative	5. Behaviorally antiprocreative
6. Self-mastery develops virtue	6. Controls biology, creates dependency

NFP: A Special Language of Love

After all the above assertions have been made, there remains one authoritative source: married couples themselves. Research from the Couple to Couple League Study (1985) and the NCCB Nationwide Study (1989)[8] reveals that natural family planning couples are the best witnesses to its effectiveness and its positive value and impact on marital intimacy.

Many couples will admit that NFP requires growth in self-control, self-sacrifice, dying to self, and other virtues needed by those who wish to follow Christ. Since marriage is a Christian sacrament, couples can discover the redeeming love of Christ by bearing his cross in *all* aspects of their life, including the periodic challenge of continence. Seen in this light, genital abstinence or continence is not merely a strategy or a technique for avoiding conception. It is a necessity for subduing one's tendency toward selfishness and for developing the virtue of self-mastery.

Far from being antisexual, continence enables a couple to embrace intercourse as a special language of total and reciprocal self-giving. Research also shows that couples who abandon contraceptives for fertility-acceptance methods are the most adamant about the difference between the two lifestyles. They see their contraceptive-free life as being filled with faith in God the Creator who enables them to love each other and their children more deeply.

This outlook fully supports the prophetic concern of the Church for the integrity of marital intercourse and fertility acceptance. Church teaching has highlighted the values of "dialogue, reciprocal respect, shared responsibility, and self-control." To this should be added the qualities of mutuality, intimacy, and bonding. These values are involved not only in the effectiveness and acceptance of the natural family planning lifestyle but also in sacramental marriage.

The Church has come under some criticism for its teaching on contraception, most notably the 1968 encyclical by Pope Paul VI called *On the Regulation of Birth* (*Humanae Vitae*). Church teaching has been misrepresented or misunderstood in and outside the Church. It has been our hope that, through this booklet, you are able to have a better understanding of the values that inform Church teaching on marriage and the gift of fertility. A British author, commenting on the importance of that teaching, sums up this section well:

> If the pope had accepted artificial contraception, he would
> have encouraged couples to import the profane techno-

logical mentality into the most sacred and private of human spheres. On the other hand, natural family planing, by means of cyclic abstinence, respects the sacred, respects woman, and respects nature....It treats sex as a path to wholeness, because wholeness is achieved by self-giving and self-giving depends on self-possession. NFP can be used as a way of taking possession of our sexuality, whereas, contraception is merely a way of avoiding consequences. The two paths lead in different directions.[9]

Notes

1. *The Documents Of Vatican II, Pastoral Constitution on the Church in the Modern World,* #51, America Press, New York, NY, 1966.
2. Ibid., #48.
3. Pope John Paul II, *On the Family (Familiaris Consortio),* Part Two, #11.
4. M. Fightlin, *International Review of Natural Family Planning,* Vol. IX, #2, Summer 1985, p. 129.
5. Ronald Lawler, O.F.M. Cap., Joseph Boyle, and William E. May, *Catholic Sexual Ethics,* Our Sunday Visitor, Inc., Huntington, IN, 1996, p. 161.
6. Donald DeMarco, *International Review of Natural Family Planning,* Vol. X, Spring 1986, p. 67.
7. Pope John Paul II, op. cit., Part Two, #32.
8. Diocesan Development Program for Natural Family Planning Nationwide Study (1989). National Conference of Catholic Bishops, Dr. Grace Boys, Coordinator. (Analyzed responses of over 3300 NFP users. For a copy of the study, contact the DDP office of the NCCB, 202-541-3240.)
9. Stratford Caldecott, "On the 'Greenness' of Catholicism and Its Further 'Greening,'" in *New Oxford Review,* Vol. LIII, #10, 1989, p. 11.

Seeking the Truth and Embracing It

In our secular culture, the birth-control issue often is looked upon with a rather pragmatic attitude of "use what is most effective no matter the cost." The prevalence of abortion-on-demand, often as a backup for contraceptive failure, is a reflection of this attitude. While a Christian attitude includes the need for being responsible, this notion of responsibility does not derive simply from "common sense" or an attitude of the "end justifies the means." The Christian attitude toward contraception and family planning derives from what we are called to do and who we are called to become in Christ. Decisions about family planning must be situated in this faith context.

For the Catholic Christian, conscience is formed by prayerful reflection on the pertinent scriptural passages and Church teachings that serve as the primary indicators of God's will. A well-formed conscience enables us to make responsible decisions by seeking the truth and embracing it. This section assumes that, for those who are seriously probing the Christian meaning of marital sexuality, Church teaching is not merely one option among a variety of value systems. Rather, Church teaching is the fundamental basis of conscience formation.

In the context of marriage, the Church views sexuality as an essential part of the way a human being establishes the most intimate and basic relationships in life: the relationship to (1) one's own body and emotions, (2) one's spouse, and (3) the next generation in procreation.

These relationships are revelatory; they reveal something about God. We are God's children, and the relationships within the Trinity—Father, Son, and Holy Spirit—are analogous to a family of love. Therefore, the Church is not concerned just with sex for its own sake; it is concerned with sex as a central dimension in the network of human life, and it views sexual ethics as critical to the living of a Christian life. Sexual ethics is an essential dimension of the ethics of authentic love.

With these points in mind, let us take a brief look at how the Church defines responsible parenthood, one of the important callings of sacramental marriage. We will also touch on conscience formation and moral decision making.

Responsible Parenthood

In the encyclical *On the Regulation of Birth (Humanae Vitae)*, Pope Paul VI identifies four "aspects" of responsible parenthood:

1. The "knowledge and respect of" reproductive processes which are integral parts of the human person;
2. The integration of the "tendencies of instinct or passion" with our reason and free will;
3. Consideration of the "physical, economic, psychological and social conditions" in relation to which couples generously decide to have several children or, for serious reasons, to limit their family size;
4. A "profound relationship" with the moral order established by God, through the formation of a "right conscience."[1]

Responsible parenthood implies that couples take into account many different factors when having a family, including the on-going fruitfulness involved in educating and raising children. In the transmission of life, Catholics are not free to disregard the creative intentions of God. The complementary nature of man and woman, the sex drive and the reproductive faculty, the desire for love and unity—all are mysteries to be lived. These are connected "perspectives" of human relationships, and the transmission of life is an important component. This is why the Church teaches that married couples are to respect this gift and the meaning it has in their overall relationship.

How many children should you responsibly seek to parent? The bishops of the Second Vatican Council address this challenging question. In the *Pastoral Constitution on the Church in the Modern World,* they remind married couples that family planning decisions cannot be made arbitrarily or simply on the basis of convenience. Family planning requires decisions of conscience that must respect the law of God and the teaching authority of the Church which authentically interprets divine law. When Christian couples, in a spirit of sacrifice and with trust in divine Providence, carry out their duties of procreation with generous, human, and Christian responsibility, they glorify the Creator and find fulfillment in Christ.[2]

In forming your conscience, you need to reflect carefully upon the teaching of the Church as normative for the Catholic Christian.

Conscience Formation

The tradition of the Church emphasizes two key aspects of conscience: "(1) as absolutely fundamental in understanding the dignity of the human person in his or her relationship with God, and (2) as a practical moral guide in making judgments and decisions in daily life."[3] We are called as individuals and as couples to image God's love by the free, mutual, and responsible giving of ourselves to each other. For "God does not force the human person to live responsibly and lovingly, but he does invite and call in the depths of each person's heart. Here, 'in the depths of the heart,' is where conscience exists....The dignity of the human person is this: that he or she can intelligently and *freely* choose God's will and God's law."[4]

The American Catholic bishops are aware of the complex nature of the family planning issue and the many reasons people reject Church teaching on the subject. This is why in 1976 the American bishops issued a statement of concern, which said in part: "We ask our people not to lose heart or turn away from the community of faith when they find themselves caught in these conflicts. We urge them to seek appropriate and understanding pastoral counsel, to make use of God's help in constant prayer and recourse to the sacraments, and to investigate honestly such legitimate methods of birth limitation as natural family planning."[5]

The above quotation is out of context here, and is neither a substitute nor a basis for conscience formation. It has been quoted to show that the pastoral leaders of the Church are aware of the difficulty in living up to the call. Conscience formation is a lifelong process, of which moral decision making is a major part. In fact, good moral decision making is the goal, the end result, of a well-formed conscience. When it comes to marriage and family life, there are many moral decisions involved in the way you as husband and wife love each other, relate with your children, handle your finances, and so on.

Conscience development is important in order that moral decision making occurs in a correct, reasonable manner. Your conscience is to be formed throughout your life. Time, prayer, consultation, humility, and honesty are required so that you are always seeking the truth of what is best—what is God's will for human life in a given situation.

Conscience can be defined as "one's best judgment as to what, in the circumstances, is the morally right thing to do...it cannot merely be a feeling or a personal decision to act or live in a certain way....Concern for the truth is essential....But conscience does more than reveal the gap between what we are and what we ought to become. It is also a summons to realize our full humanity.

"For one who has Catholic faith, who has acquired a happy, personal certainty that the Lord teaches and guides us in the teaching of the Church, the insistent message of the Catholic faith is not something alien to conscience....Church teaching is there from the beginning in the formation of conscience."[6]

Following is a brief presentation on the steps involved in moral decision making, which is the result of a well-formed conscience.

Steps in Moral Decision Making

1. Define the problem and the effects it is having on persons or situations in your life.
2. Prayerfully study, respect, and heed the guidance of the Church in the matter.
3. Examine the alternatives.
4. Take counsel with several people of various stages and experience in life—people you trust, people who will be truthful and objective with you, perhaps even confrontative.
5. Pray for guidance, humility, wisdom, and mercy.
6. Judge which alternative is morally right. Then choose to do it.
7. Resolve to continue praying about the decision.

It is important to realize that moral decision making is not an overnight process; forming your conscience takes time and must become a pattern in your life. Conscience formation and moral decision making should open you up to yourself. There is a difference between looking for an answer and looking for a justification for what you "feel" is right or have already decided to do. The ongoing formation of your conscience means that you are sincerely open to continuing the inquiry.

Notes

1. Pope Paul VI, *On the Regulation of Birth* (the encyclical *Humanae Vitae,* on marriage and responsible parenthood), 1968, #10.
2. *The Documents of Vatican II, Pastoral Constitution on the Church in the Modern World,* #50.
3. Daniel L. Lowery, C.SS.R., *Following Christ: A Handbook of Catholic Moral Teaching,* Liguori Publications, 1982, p. 39.
4. Ibid., pp. 39-40.
5. National Conference of Catholic Bishops, *To Live in Christ Jesus: A Pastoral Reflection on the Moral Life,* 1976, II.
6. Lawler, Boyle, and May, *Catholic Sexual Ethics,* pp. 100, 112.

Worksheet

Directions: Make two photocopies of this worksheet—one for each partner. Take ten to fifteen minutes *apart* from each other. Reflect on the questions and jot down your honest response to each. Then take time together to review and discuss your answers. (Write your answers on a separate sheet of paper or on the copy of this page.)

1. I hope we will have _____ number of children.

2. How would I like us to achieve our family size?

3. How will I/we know when we are ready to have children/start a family?

4. Who is responsible for our avoiding or achieving pregnancy in our marriage? Me? my spouse? a doctor?

5. If, in spite of our best efforts to avoid conception, we became pregnant, I would (think, feel, do, and so on)...

6. If I found out we were unable to conceive and bear children, I would (think, feel, do, and so on)...

7. What is the relationship between our family planning decision and our Christian faith?

8. Do I feel we both have a good grasp of all forms of family planning? Do I feel at peace about our family planning decisions? Explain.

Additional Resources

Billings, Lyn and Westinore, Ann. *The Billings Method: Controlling Fertility Without Drugs or Devices.* Lewiston, NY: Life Cycle Books, 2000.

Catechism of the Catholic Church. United States Catholic Conference, Inc.—Libreria Editrice Vaticana, 1994. www.christusrex.org/www2/kerygma/ccc/searchcat.html

DeMarco, Donald. *New Perspectives on Contraception.* Dayton, OH: One More Soul, 1999.

Joyce, Mary R. *Women and Choice: A New Beginning.* St. Cloud, MN: LifeCom, 1985.

Kippley, John F. *Sex and the Marriage Covenant: A Basis for Morality.* Cincinnati: The Couple to Couple League International, Inc., 1991. www.ccli.org

Kippley, John F. and Sheila K. *The Art of Natural Family Planning* (4th ed.). Cincinnati: The Couple to Couple League International, Inc., 1996. www.ccli.org

Klaus, Hanna. *Natural Family Planning: A Review* (2nd ed.). Bethesda, MD: Natural Family Planning Center, 1995.

Pope Paul VI. *Humanae Vitae.* United States Catholic Conference, 1968.

Shivanandan, Mary. *Crossing the Threshold of Love: A New Vision of Marriage in the Light of John Paul II's Anthropology.* Washington, DC: Catholic University of America Press, 1999. http://cuapress.cua.edu/books.html

Smith, Janet E., editor. *Why* Humanae Vitae *Was Right: A Reader.* San Francisco: Ignatius Press, 1993.

United States Catholic Conference. *Human Sexuality: A Catholic Perspective for Education and Lifelong Learning.* Washington, DC, 1990.

West, Christopher. *The Good News About Sex and Marriage: Answers to Your Honest Questions About Catholic Teaching.* Ann Arbor, MI: Servant Publications, 2000. www.omsoul.com

Wilson, Mercedes Arzu. *Love and Fertility: How to Avoid or Achieve Pregnancy...Naturally!* Dunkirk, MD: Family of the Americas Foundation, 1992.

Winstein, Merryl. *Your Fertility Signals: Using Them to Achieve or Avoid Pregnancy, Naturally.* St. Louis: Smooth Stone Press, 1998.

Wright, Wendy M. *Sacred Dwelling: A Spirituality of Family Life* (2nd ed.). Leavenworth, KS: Forest of Peace Publishing, 1994.

NFP Resource Centers

In the United States:

**Billings Ovulation
  Method Association (OM)**
P.O. Box 16206
St. Paul, MN 55116
(651) 699-8139
www.boma-usa.org
www.woomb.org

**The Couple to Couple
  League (S-T)**
3621 Glenmore Avenue
P.O. Box 11084
Cincinnati, OH 45211
(513) 661-7612
www.ccli.org

**Family of the Americas
  Foundation, Inc.**
P.O. Box 1170
Dunkirk, MD 20754
(301) 627-3346
www.familyplanning.net

**Northwest Family
  Services, Inc. (S-T)**
4805 Northeast Glisan Street
Portland, OR 97213
(503) 230-6377
www.nwfs.org

One More Soul
616 Five Oaks
Dayton, OH 45406
(800) 307-SOUL
www.omsoul.com

**Pope Paul vi Institute
  for the Study of Human
  Reproduction (OM)**
6901 Mercy Road
Omaha, NE 68106
(402) 390-6600
www.creightonmodel.com

**Diocesan Development
  Program for NFP**
USCCB
3211 Fourth Stree NE
Washington, DC 20017-1194
(202) 341-3070 or 3240
www.usccb.org/prolife/
issues/nfp/index.htm

In Canada:

SERENA Canada
6239 Chemin Peacon
Montreal, Quebec H3S 2P6
Canada
www.serena.ca/eng/start.html